Who would want those apples anyway?

By Laura and Pam Griscom

Illustrated by T. Scot Halpin

Share Publishing, Portola Valley, California

Who would want those apples anyway?

By Laura and Pam Griscom
Illustrated by T. Scot Halpin

Published and Distributed by:
Share Publishing   Phone: 408-867-0337
P.O. Box 263, Saratoga, CA 95071

For information about agricultural pesticides, contact:
Pesticide Education Center
P.O. Box 420870, San Francisco, CA 94142
415-391-8511
or
United Farmworkers of America
AFL-CIO, La Paz, Keene, CA 93570
805-822-5571

Many thanks to Michael Halperin at Frazer Lake Farms, Hollister, California

© Laura and Pam Griscom (Text)
© T. Scot Halpin (Illustration)
All rights reserved
1st Printing 1994
Printed in the United States of America
ISBN 0-99633075-3-7 4.95
Bookland EAN 9 780963 370532

"In the end we will conserve only what we love; we will love only what we understand; and we will understand only what we are taught."

Baba Dioum (Senegal)

Laura's tomato plants were growing fast. She checked on them every day.

When the first tomatoes were big and juicy, Laura picked them for her family to eat. "Your tomatoes are delicious!" said her mommy, her daddy, and her big sister Bailey. Laura felt very proud.

One day Laura noticed that some pieces were missing from a tomato that was still growing. "What could have happened to it?" she asked Bailey.

"Let's ask our friend Michael," said Bailey. "He'll know what happened because he's a farmer."

Michael's farm was very big, but his plants looked comfortable and happy. He was growing lots of different vegetables at his farm. His friends, the ladybugs, thought it was a nice place to live.

Michael found one plant that had some little pieces missing, just like Laura's tomato. He explained that a bug had taken some bites out of it. "My helpful ladybugs keep lots of the problem bugs away," he said, "but sometimes a problem bug sneaks in and takes some bites when the ladybugs aren't looking."

"Don't you know how to keep all the plants safe?!" asked Laura.

"Well..." Michael answered. "I know that some farmers put strong poisons called pesticides on their plants. They want to kill every bug that comes to their farm. But pesticides can poison people too. So, I don't use them. I am an organic farmer."

When Laura got home she looked and looked at her tomato plants. She didn't like the bug marks. But she didn't want to put poison on her yummy tomatoes. Laura thought about her problem for a long time. Then she turned to Bailey and announced...

"It's okay if the bugs share with us. They have very *teeny* little teeth.

A few weeks later, Laura went to play with her friend Rosa. Rosa's daddy picks apples, and her family lives in a little house next to an apple orchard.

Laura thought the orchard was wonderful. She and Rosa played in the apple trees. "You're lucky to live near an orchard," Laura said.

But Rosa started to look sad. "Sometimes it's scary here," she said. "Why?!" asked Laura.

"Sometimes they spray pesticides on the trees," Rosa answered. "Then we can't go outside for a whole day. And last year they sprayed our house by mistake. My brother got sick and couldn't breathe. He had to go to the hospital." Suddenly, Rosa stopped talking and looked around. Then she whispered, "I'm not really supposed to talk about it. If the apple growers hear me, we won't be able to live here anymore."

That night, Laura told her family about the people who kept putting poison on the trees near Rosa's house. She wished they would stop. "Why don't they share with the bugs?" she asked.

"The farmers want to sell more of their apples," her mommy answered. "They use pesticides and other chemicals to make all their apples look the same and to be sure there are never any bites missing. They think shoppers will like them better that way."

"Don't they care if the people who work for them get sick?" asked Bailey.
"Some farmers just don't seem to notice," said Mommy sadly.

"But who would want those apples anyway?" asked Laura. "Doesn't everyone know that poison is bad to eat?!"
"I don't know," Mommy replied. "Maybe people don't realize that some of the poison is still on the food when they eat it, or that the chemicals also poison the earth we live on and the water we drink."

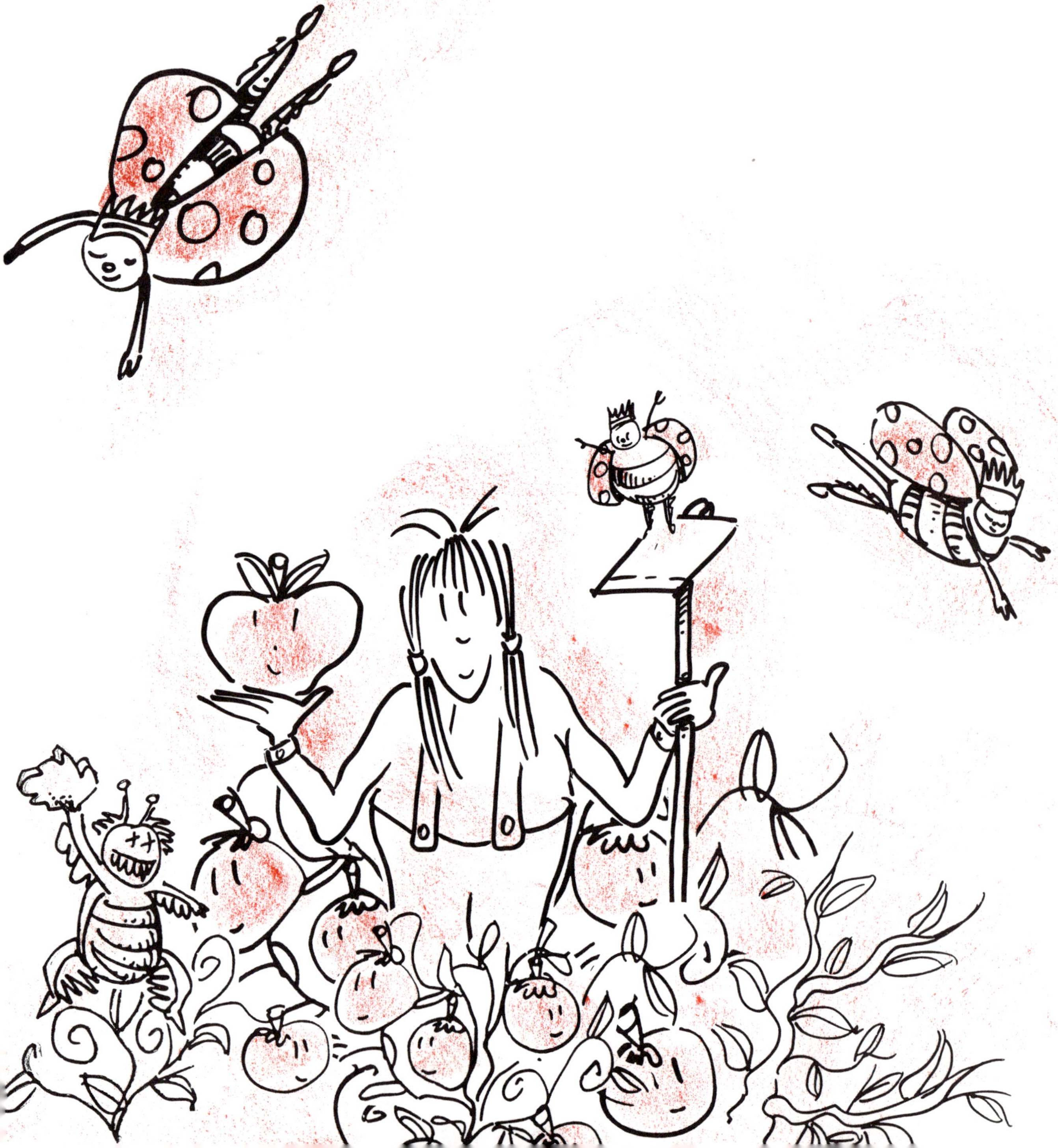

"Bugs know all about that," said Laura. "They never choose food from chemical farms. Bugs are very smart."

The next day, Laura and Bailey went to the grocery store with their daddy. They noticed that some kinds of fruit and vegetables were very shiny and that each one looked just the same as all the others in their pile.

Then they noticed that some piles of fruit and vegetables were all a little bit different from each other. "These are organic," Daddy explained. "Each one looks different, just like each person looks different. Being different is natural."

Laura and Bailey saw that something had taken a tiny bite out of one of the organic pears. They became *very* excited. "Daddy, Daddy," they squealed, "please choose the same pears the bug chose!"

Their daddy filled a big basket with organic pears.

"Nobody got sick from chemicals where these pears were grown," said Laura happily. "And we won't have to *eat* any poison when we eat them," added Bailey.

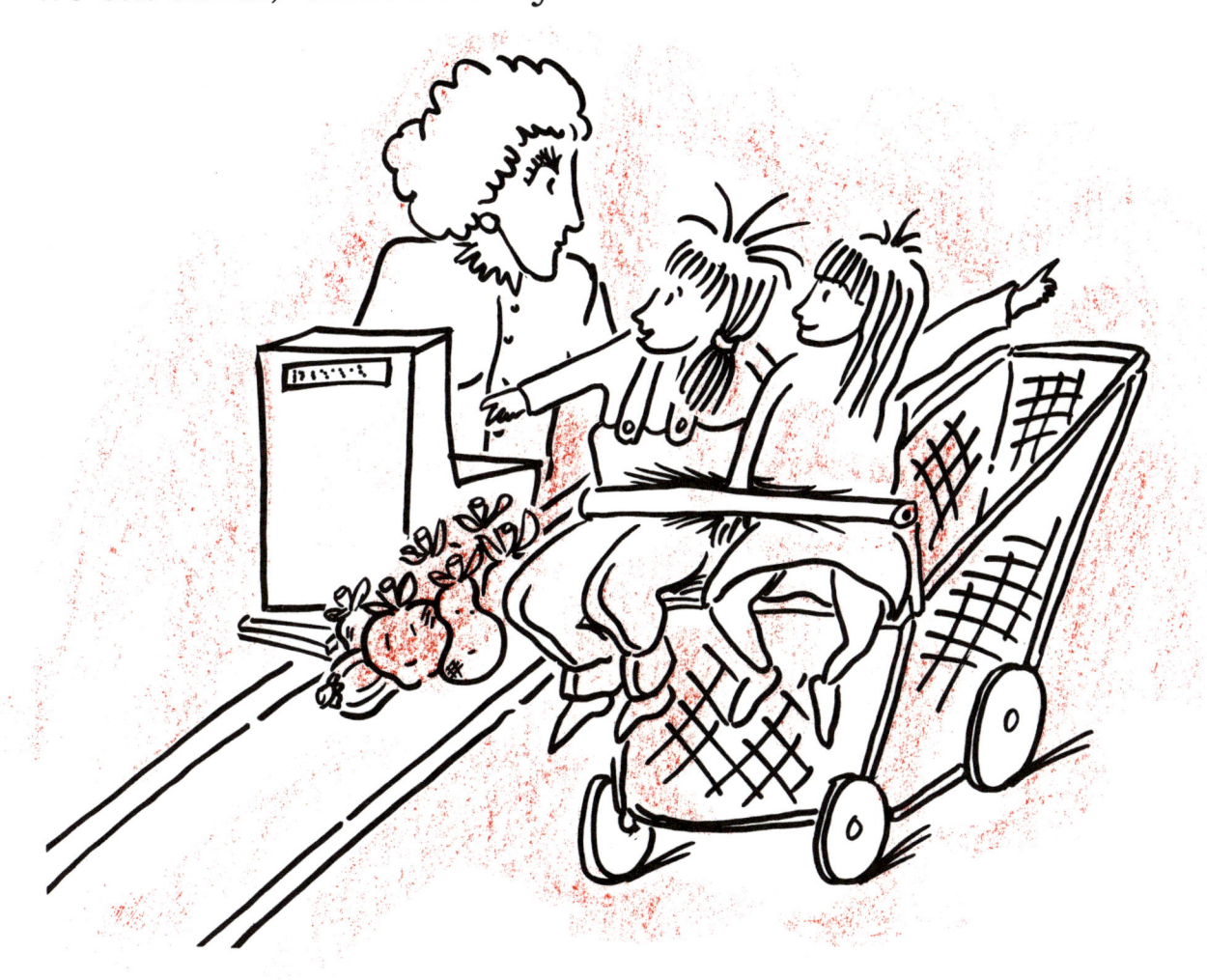

"Look!!" said Laura to the cashier. "We're getting lots of organic stuff! You can tell the farmers we don't need any more of the poisoned kind."

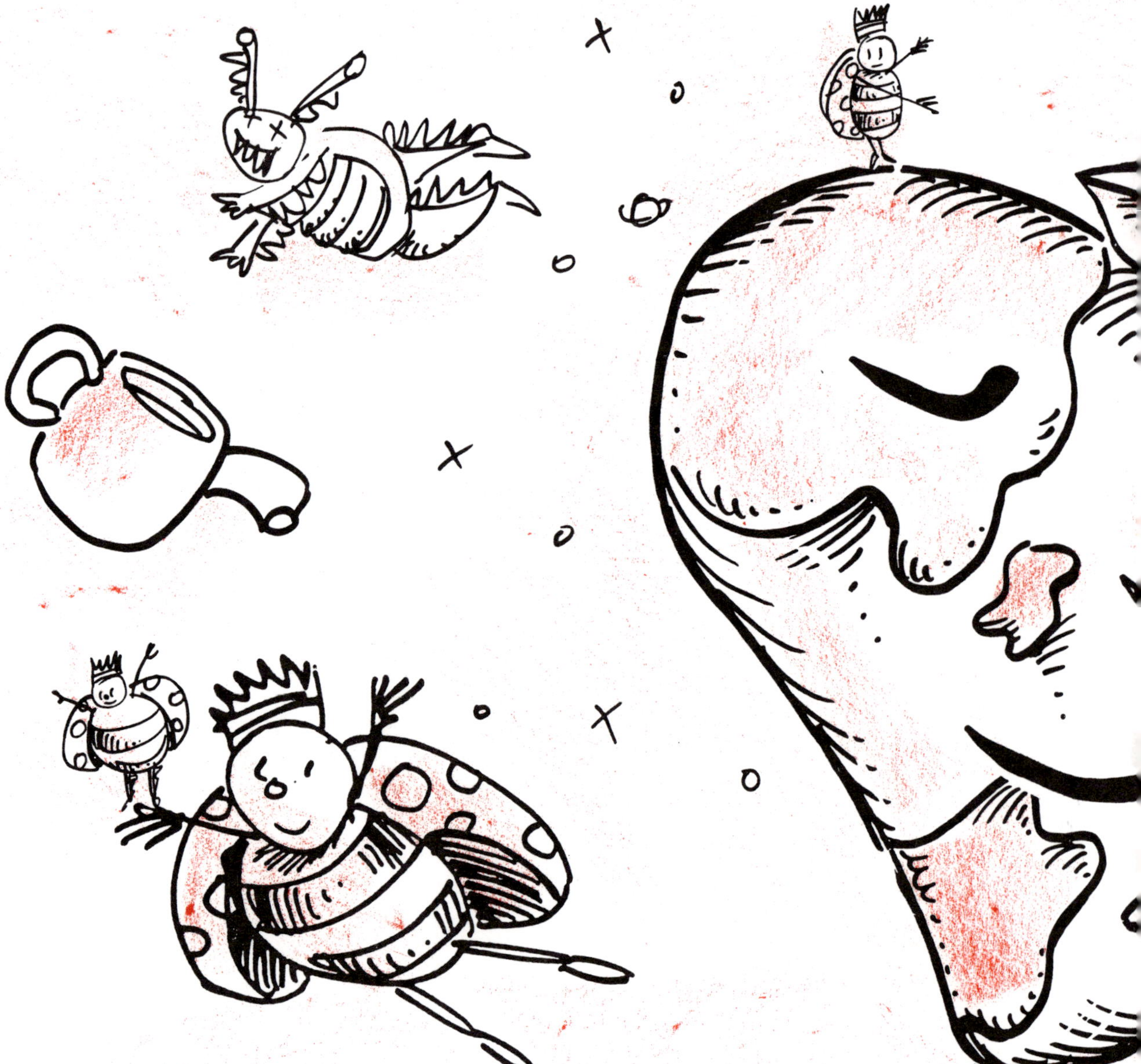

What will you tell the farmers?